A Three Element Social Skill Program

A Three Element Social Skill Program:
Instruction, Drama, & Technology

Michelle Henderson, M. Ed.

Copyright © 2009 by Michelle Henderson

All rights reserved. No part of this book may be reproduced, stored, or transmitted by any means—whether auditory, graphic, mechanical, or electronic—without written permission of both publisher and author, except in the case of brief excerpts used in critical articles and reviews. Unauthorized reproduction of any part of this work is illegal and is punishable by law.

ISBN: 978-0-578-02498-1

Dedication

I want to dedicate this book to everyone who makes a difference in a child's life. Being an educator, I have witnessed teachers working long hours to meet the needs of their students. When teachers work hard to develop an environment that makes learning fun for their students, the smile on the children faces becomes the award.

I want to thank the Lewisville ISD for the training I received that enabled me to grow as the best teacher that I could become. I also want to thank Lake Dallas ISD for allowing me to create and implement the three-element social skill program that this book endorses.

The social skill program also would not have been developed without the students who attend IASIS Learning Center. These students have been a joy to teach! They amaze me with their creativity, and willingness to take chances.

This book would not have been possible without the support from my husband and family! Dreams can be accomplished if the people you love believe and support you!

Many Blessings!
Michelle Henderson

Contents

Author's Note		ix
Chapter 1:	A Three Element Social Skill Program	1
Chapter 2:	Social Skill Evaluations	7
Chapter 3:	Social-Skill Lessons Conversations and Getting to Know Others	29
Chapter 4:	Social Skill Lesson: Identifying Feelings in Self and in Others	41
Chapter 5:	Social Skill Lesson: How to Deal with a Bullying Attempt	51
Chapter 6:	Social Skill Lesson: Preparing for Vocational and Career Plans	55

Author's Note

"All the world's a stage!" When reflecting different relationships that people are involved in, everyone plays different parts. A woman can play a daughter, sister, wife, and mother. Relationships can be difficult for anyone if he does not know what role he is in.

Our world can be a confusing place for children who display social deficits. Educators and parents should be able to celebrate a child's uniqueness and individual talents. Utilizing creativity can bring out self-expression that many children need to share with others. Drama techniques and visual media are concrete methods that can be used to teach children strategies and techniques to learn important social skills. Children should view the world as a stage for <u>them</u>. They can play any role that they choose to play, and their dreams can be accomplished if they have enough self-esteem and support from others.

The term "educators" is used throughout this book. Educators are those who work with children on a daily basis. This includes parents, teachers, and therapist. Please copy anything in the book that you need to use to help your students. I hope that you will be able to create your own social skill program that your students will benefit from. Everyone makes a difference in a child's life.

Chapter 1:

A Three Element Social Skill Program

Creativity is inventing, experimenting, growing, taking risks, breaking rules, making mistakes, and having fun.

~ Mary Lou Cook

Our schools have seen many changes through recent years. As the needs of society have changed, so has the philosophy of our education systems. Not only have the needs of students changed with each passing decade, but so has the teaching techniques that are being used in the classrooms. Technology has made our lives easier, but with every change, there are always challenges. The new millennium has introduced us to life-like video games, cell phones, music storage devices, and the ability to communicate instantly with almost anyone. In effect, classroom teachers now have to be more creative to keep the students of today interested in learning.

Many children that are attending our public and private schools have difficulty communicating and interacting with their peers because they don't understand some of the basic social behaviors that others learn naturally. They may have been diagnosed with Autism Spectrum Disorders or other learning disorders that can lend themselves toward social deficits. These disorders often interfere with the learning process. If these students do not understand the social rules of learning, many problems will arise. They will have difficulty developing relationships with teachers and other students. Their self-esteem can suffer as they become frustrated. Many of them will be seen as a behavior problem. As we strive to educate children, our goal should be to prepare them for an independent life once they have graduated from high school. If their social deficits are not addressed, they may have trouble preparing for a chosen career.

In order for a student with social deficits to be successful in school, with relationships, and with career choices it is vital to address these problems in an educational setting. There is an ample amount of material that teachers can use to integrate a social skill curriculum into the school day. Before any teaching intervention takes place, however, the teacher should collect data about the student's behavior. Fresh behavioral data must also be collected throughout the intervention. A thorough behavioral analysis is essential in order to determine whether the interventions are effective or in need of modification.

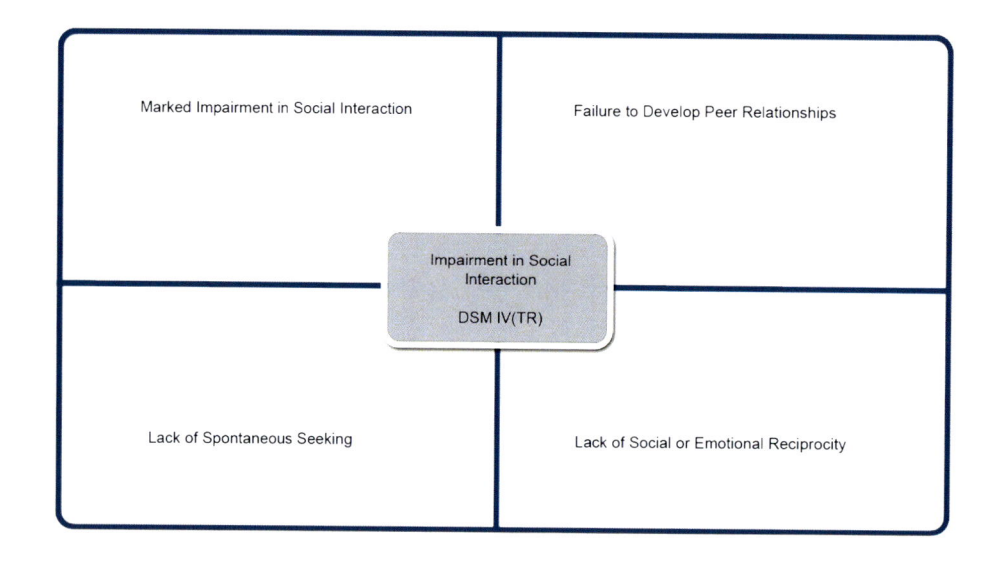

```
+--------------------------------------+--------------------------------------+
| Marked Impairment in Social          | Failure to Develop Peer              |
| Interaction                          | Relationships                        |
|                                      |                                      |
|              Impairment in Social Interaction              |
|                       DSM IV(TR)                           |
|                                      |                                      |
| Lack of Spontaneous Seeking          | Lack of Social or Emotional          |
|                                      | Reciprocity                          |
+--------------------------------------+--------------------------------------+
```

The above table illustrates the diagnostic social interaction criteria of a student who has been diagnosed with Asperger's Disorder. To meet this criterion, a student must display two out of the four social interaction deficits. The professionals that are tasked with developing educational goals for this student should develop a social skill intervention program that will address these areas, as well as a behavioral analysis in order to determine which interventions should be followed.

This manual uses three primary elements that will assist the educator in developing a social skill program designed to improve their students' social deficits.

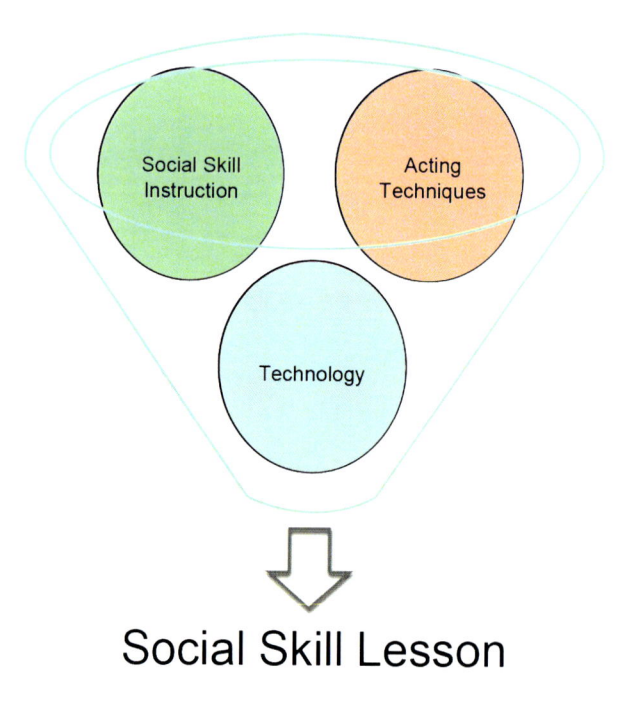

- Social Skill Instruction
- Acting Techniques
- Technology

⇩

Social Skill Lesson

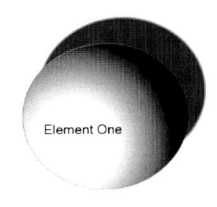

Social Skill Instruction

Element One

Educators should begin creating a social skill program by adopting a curriculum, which includes the following:

- A menu of social skills.
- A list of different teaching modalities (visual, motor, and auditory) and activities for each social skill.
- Explanation of how to generalize the strategies learned for different social environments.

Social skill instruction is direct instruction. It includes modeling behavior, rehearsal, role-playing, and coaching. These strategies help improve a student's communication, problem solving, decision making, self-management, and peer-relations. The goal of effective social skill instruction is to provide positive behavior support for the school, home, and community.

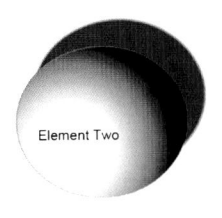

Using Acting with Social Skill Instruction

Element Two

"Drama activities can teach body language, facial expression, tone of voice, and provide an opportunity for a young person with Asperger's Syndrome to act and rehearse responses to specific situations, such as teasing."

Tony Attwood 2007

As an actor practices and hones his skills, he becomes increasingly aware of his own feelings and emotions. As he learns to "walk in the shoes of another", he develops a heightened sense of empathy for those that he portrays. He also must learn to regulate the intonations and inflections of his voice and to control his body movements as he slips into his assigned role. As you integrate some of these acting techniques into your social skills lessons, the added benefit for the student includes an increase in self-awareness and self-esteem.

Many students that display undeveloped social abilities are not actively involved in recreational sports or leisure activities. As educators introduce acting techniques into their lessons, the students will begin to realize how important recreational and leisure activities through the fine arts can be. These lessons can be structured to help them learn how to improvise in social situations, create and deliver speeches and stories, interview their peers, perform skits, and develop their own news segment or cooking show.

A Three Element Social Skill Program

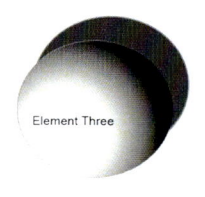

Using Technology with Social Skill Instruction

A dynamic and creative social skill lesson can be made more effective by adding some fun and engaging technologic effects. For a very modest investment, a teacher can easily set up a small studio that will enhance the social skills lessons by reinforcing the "acting techniques" angle. With this simple studio, a teacher can produce multiple personalized video clips, which demonstrate a specific set of social behaviors that the student can view and practice with repeatedly. Developing and practicing with individualized video-modeling clips can increase the chances that the learned social skill behaviors will generalize to different environments

Some of the equipment that will be needed is shown below.

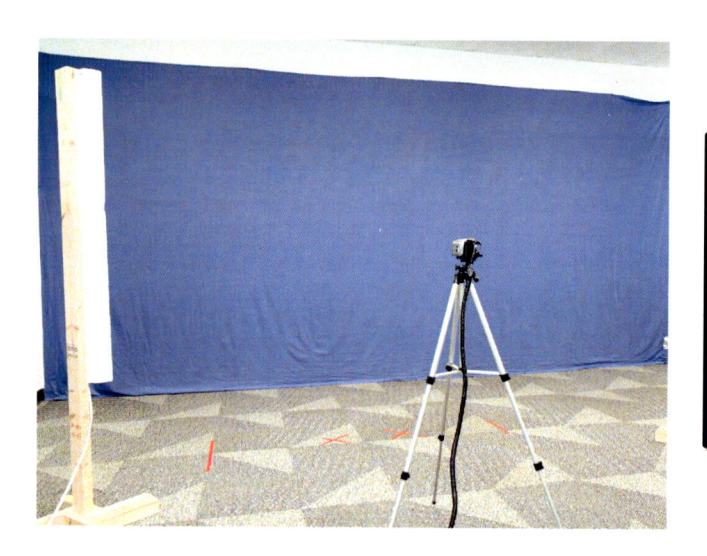

1. A blue or green background
2. A home video camera
3. Studio lighting
4. A video mixer (for real-time results)
5. Video editing software with a chroma key effect feature

By taking advantage of movie-making technologies, students can pretend to travel to anyplace their imaginations want to take them. They can act within the setting of a school, a castle, a forest, or even a video game. Educators can also use these techniques to develop individual social skill video clips of appropriate behaviors, as well as to create stories from the students' point of view.

These types of videos are made possible by using a studio effect called "chroma key". The most popular and most common use of the chroma key effect that most people would recognize occurs when you watch your daily weather report. The reporter is not actually standing in front of a map that shows your local weather, but is in fact standing in front of a solid blue or green background. Then the studio uses video mixing equipment to remove the solid color and overlay the image of the weather reporter on top of a computerized video image of a weather map. You can use this same technology in your lessons by producing video clips on your own computer, or live and in "real-time" with a modest video mixer and television monitor.

Green or blue chroma key fabric or paint can be purchased relatively inexpensively. When you record your students in front of this background, they should not be wearing any clothing that is the same color as the screen. You should also take care to ensure that the color of any props that are used in the scene contrast with the background. The colors blue and green are most commonly used because they are considered to be least like our skin tone. The choice between green and blue is not as important as verifying that the video mixer or software that you will be using is capable of matching the color of the background. Green is often preferred because the clothing that a typical student wears is more likely to contain elements of blue than of green.

The quality of the chroma key effect in your finished product will be directly related to the attention that you give to lighting the scene properly. Professional studio lighting can be very expensive, fragile, and bulky. A trip to your local hardware store, however, can supply you with substitutes that will yield more than adequate results. Remember, the videos you produce do not have to be professional or error free for your students to enjoy them.

An Example of Chroma-Keying

To properly light your studio set, you must concentrate on both the background and the foreground. The background lighting must evenly illuminate your background screen without shadows, hot spots, or dark areas. This is critical in order for the chroma key effect to look believable. This can be accomplished by using two or more halogen lights. You will need to devote some time to experimenting with the number, brightness, and placement of lights on your background until the best possible result is achieved.

The foreground lighting will need to be focused on the subjects and props in the scene. It must be noted that the color of the foreground lighting can dramatically affect the look of the subjects in the video. One cost effective option for foreground lighting is to use shop lights with fluorescent bulbs that are optimized for use in aquariums. These bulbs have a high color rendering index (CRI at 87 or above), and will reproduce skin tone colors more accurately than standard fluorescent bulbs. If you do use fluorescent shop lights, be sure to only use those with an electronic ignition. Fixtures equipped with magnetic ignition emit an annoying hum that will be obvious on the audio track of your video.

This picture illustrates how you can create your own studio lights.

> Inexpensive lighting can be constructed from standard 2 x 4 wood studs, and a standard fluorescent shop light with electronic ignition.

Although a video mixer and television monitor are not required in the production of these video clips, the additional expense will greatly enhance any social skills lesson where acting techniques are used. Adding these two pieces of equipment will allow the student to visualize how the finished video will look and to provide immediate feedback for reinforcing the lesson. It can be very helpful for a student to be able to watch themselves as they role-play and create different scenes. Some students may become uncomfortable or agitated while watching themselves during the playback of pre-recorded videos. Watching themselves in "real-time" can help them to develop a sense of self-awareness, while repeatedly watching recorded clips will help them generalize the learned social skill.

Video modeling and video self-modeling (video clips where children see themselves performing desired behaviors) are both effective in targeting social skills and functional skills, according to recent studies. In addition, the researchers found that improvements were maintained after the program was concluded and skills were transferred to other settings not featured on the videos. (IU News Room; Indiana University, 2007)

Another great way to enhance social skill lessons with technology is to incorporate DVDs or interactive computer software that use video modeling to teach the appropriate strategies used in various social situations. You can also use video clips from popular movies with which the student is familiar. While the student is watching a social scenario from one of their favorite movies, pause the video to allow him to study the different facial expressions, body language, and feelings that occur. This will help them learn to analyze the personality of the character and to determine if the character is following the "social rules".

If you plan to use commercially available movies on DVD or video cassette, be aware that you may need to purchase a public performance license. DVD and video cassette movies are usually licensed only for private home viewing. Any other use will most likely require a license. Some allowances are made for educational use in schools, but you should check with your school administration or librarian to verify whether your school is covered by a public performance license.

Chapter 2:

Social Skill Evaluations

As teachers, we must constantly try to improve schools and we must keep working at changing and experimenting and trying until we have developed ways of reaching every child.

~ Albert Shanker

Before you can design a program to teach social skills, the student's social strengths and deficits must be evaluated. Observing the student across settings is the best informal social evaluation that you can complete. Observe younger students on the playground, in the cafeteria, in the classroom, and during unstructured time. Older students should be observed in class, in the cafeteria, and during any transition activity at school. The evaluator can then determine how this student interacts with others and how he is able to self-regulate during social interactions.

Interviewing the student's teachers and parents can provide the educator with vital information. Surveys and questionnaires that help to evaluate social abilities are commercially available. The educator should interview the student as well, in order to determine how the student interacts with others on an individual basis. The data collected should be analyzed at a later time. After collecting the answers and feedback from the surveys and interviews, the information can be organized and developed into a list of stated goals to address the student's social deficits.

Using emotion or facial expression cards, an educator can determine the student's ability to interpret non-verbal language and to understand his own emotions. Situational cards assist in evaluating the student's knowledge about different social situations and understanding the "story" in the picture. You can purchase social scenario pictures, or you can just use your own family photos.

The following pages show examples of forms that an educator can use to complete an informal social skill evaluation of a student.

Student Interview

1. What is your full name? _____
2. When is your birthday? _____
3. Where do you go to school? _____
4. What grade are you in? _____
5. Who are your friends at school?
   _____
   _____

6. What do you like to do with your friends?
   _____
   _____
   _____

7. Why do you like about your friends?
   _____
   _____

8. What is your favorite activity to do at school?
   _____
   _____

9. What is your favorite activity to do at home?
   _____
   _____

10. Do your friends ever make you angry?
    _____
    _____

11. Have you ever been bullied?
    _____
    _____

12. Describe your family. What does your family like to do together?

_____
_____
_____

13. What job do you want to pursue after high school?

_____
_____
_____

14. What are you good at doing?

_____
_____
_____

15. What do you think that you need help with?

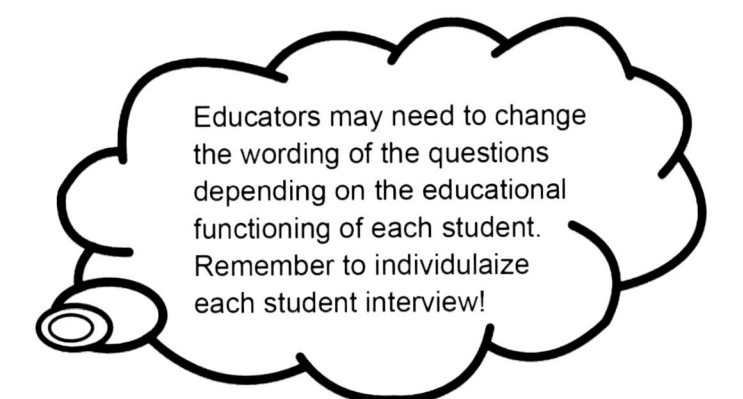

_____
_____
_____

> Educators may need to change the wording of the questions depending on the educational functioning of each student. Remember to individulaize each student interview!

A Three Element Social Skill Program

Social Situations

1. What do you think is happening in this picture?
2. What do you think the people in the picture are talking about?
3. Do you think these people are friends?
4. What do you and your friends talk about?

Notes:

1. What do you think is happening in the picture?
2. What task are they doing together?
3. Are these people friends?
4. What activities do you like to do with your family and friends?

Notes:

A Three Element Social Skill Program

1. What event is happening in this picture?
2. Is this a happy or sad event?
3. What event do you enjoy?

Notes:

Michelle Henderson

1. What event is happening in this picture?
2. Is the girl happy or sad? Why does she feel this way?
3. How old do you think the girl is?
4. Are most of your friends older or younger than you?

Notes:

A Three Element Social Skill Program

1. What is happening in this picture?
2. What is the boy doing wrong?
3. How is the boy feeling?
4. What could happen to the boy?
5. Have you ever done anything wrong?

Notes:
_____
_____
_____
_____
_____
_____
_____
_____
_____

Michelle Henderson

1. What do you think is happening in this picture?
2. How is the boy feeling?
3. Explain how you know.
4. Have you ever felt this way? What event made you feel this way?

Notes:

A Three Element Social Skill Program

1. What is happening in this picture?
2. How is the little girl feeling?
3. How do you know?
4. Have you ever felt this way?
5. Explain what made you feel this way.

Notes:

Michelle Henderson

1. What do you think is happening in this picture? Explain.
2. How is the girl feeling? Explain.
3. Do you ever feel this way?
4. Where do you think the girl is?

Notes:

A Three Element Social Skill Program

1. What is happening in this picture?
2. How do you think the man is feeling? Explain.
3. How do you think the baby is feeling? Explain.

Notes:

Michelle Henderson

1. What is happening in this picture?
2. How do you think the man is feeling?
3. Do you prefer to be alone? When?
4. Where do you think the man is?

Notes:

A Three Element Social Skill Program

1. Explain what is happening in this picture.
2. What is the girl thinking? How do you know?
3. What is the little boy thinking? How do you know?
4. What is the boy in the chair thinking?
5. What do you think will happen next?

Notes:

Michelle Henderson

Parent Questionnaire and Interview

1. Name of Student: _____

2. Date of interview: _____

3. Has your child been diagnosed by a public school system, psychologist, or a medical doctor? What was the conclusion?
   _____
   _____

4. What are your child's favorite interests or activities?
   _____
   _____

5. What does your child dislike or have difficulty with?
   _____
   _____

6. What are your child's strengths?
   _____
   _____

7. Name five things that you want your child to improve in? (school, social skills, leisure activities etc.)
   1. _____
   2. _____
   3. _____
   4. _____
   5. _____

Please complete the rating system below:

0- Never Observed
1- Sometimes (at least one time a week.)
2- Always (daily)

Questions	Rating
Speaks in an appropriate tone of voice at home.	
Introduces himself/herself without being told.	
Joins group activities without being told.	
Responds appropriately when hit or pushed by another student.	
Receives criticism well.	
Controls temper when arguing with other peers.	
Gives compliments to friends or other children in the family.	
Responds appropriately to teasing from friends or relatives of his/her own age.	
Easily changes from one activity to another.	
Acknowledges compliments or praise from friends.	
Appears lonely.	
Has low self-esteem.	
Doesn't listen to what others say.	
Shows anxiety about being with a group of peers.	
Prefers to be with adults.	
Prefers to be with peers who are younger.	
Is able to use gesture, body posture, facial expression and eye-to-eye gaze in a 1 to 1 situation.	
Can imitate an adult.	
Takes turns in conversation.	
Writes or tells imaginative stories.	
Gives a simple sequence of instructions.	
Completes assignments at home/at school.	
Participates in afterschool activities.	
Can change behavior according to the situation.	
Accepts other's point of view.	
Able to express feelings.	
Discusses future plans (jobs, colleges).	

Is there more information about your child that is vital in developing an appropriate social skill program?

_____
_____
_____
_____

Please check the following social skills that would be important for your child to have interventions for.

Social Skills	
Introducing Yourself	
Beginning a Conversation	
Ending a Conversation	
Joining in a Conversation	
Asking someone out on a date	
Giving a Compliment	
Accepting a Compliment	
Asking a Question	
Contributing to Discussions	
Setting immediate and long-term goals	
Apologizing to Someone	
Knowing Your Feelings	
Expressing Your Feelings	
Recognizing Your Feelings	
Showing Understanding of Another's Feelings	
Expressing Concern for Another	
Dealing with Your Anger	
Dealing with Another's Anger	
Dealing with Fear/Anxiety	
Using Self-Control	
Responding to Teasing	
Avoiding Trouble/Peer Pressure	
Staying Out of Fights	
Accepting Consequences	
Dealing with Accusations	
Negotiating	

Social Skills	
Dealing with Boredom	
Deciding what caused a Problem	
Making a Complaint	
Answering a Complaint	
Dealing with Losing/Failure	
Dealing with Embarrassment	
Accepting No	
Being Honest	
Completing Assignments/Projects	
Following the School Procedures/Rules	
How not to be the Rule Police	
Applying for a Job	
Completing a Job Application	
Answering Questions during a Job Interview	
Knowing how to use the Restroom	
Knowing how to Participate in Leisure/After School activities	

Teacher Questionnaire and Interview

1. Name of Student: _____
2. Date of interview: _____
3. What subject/grade do you teach? _____
4. What are this student's strengths?
   _____
   _____
   _____

5. What are this student's limitations in the classroom?
   _____
   _____
   _____

6. Is this student on grade level?
   _____

7. Name five education areas that this student needs to improve in.
   1. _____
   2. _____
   3. _____
   4. _____
   5. _____

Please complete the rating system below:

> 0- Never Observed
> 1- Sometimes (at least one time a week.)
> 2- Always (daily)

Questions	Rating
Speaks in an appropriate tone at school.	
Introduces himself/herself without being told to peers that he/she just met.	
Joins group activities without being told.	
Responds appropriately when hit or pushed by another student.	
Receives criticism well.	
Controls temper when arguing with other peers.	
Gives compliments to friends or peers.	
Responds appropriately to teasing from peers.	
Easily transitions from one activity to another.	
Acknowledges compliments or praise from peers/teachers.	
Appears lonely.	
Has low self-esteem.	
Doesn't listen to what others say.	
Shows anxiety about being with a group of peers.	
Prefers to be with adults.	
Prefers to be with peers who are younger.	
Is able to use gesture, body posture, facial expression and eye-to-eye gaze in a 1 to 1 situation.	
Can imitate an adult.	
Takes turns in a conversation.	
Writes or tells imaginative stories.	
Gives a simple sequence of instructions.	
Completes assignments at home/at school.	
Participates in afterschool activities.	
Can change behavior according to the situation.	
Accepts other's point of view.	
Able to express feelings.	
Discusses future plans (jobs, colleges).	

Is there more information about this student that is vital in developing an appropriate social skill program?

_____
_____
_____
_____

Please check the following social skills that would benefit this student's educational program.

Social Skills	
Introducing Yourself	
Beginning a Conversation	
Ending a Conversation	
Joining in a Conversation	
Working well with peers.	
Giving a Compliment	
Accepting a Compliment	
Asking a Question	
Contributing to Discussions	
Setting immediate and long-term goals	
Apologizing to Someone	
Knowing Your Feelings	
Expressing Your Feelings	
Recognizing Your Feelings	
Showing Understanding of Another's Feelings	
Expressing Concern for Another	
Dealing with Your Anger	
Dealing with Another's Anger	
Dealing with Fear/Anxiety	
Using Self-Control	
Responding to Teasing	
Avoiding Trouble/Peer Pressure	
Staying Out of Fights	
Accepting Consequences	
Dealing with Accusations	
Negotiating	

Social Skills	
Dealing with Boredom	
Deciding what caused a Problem	
Making a Complaint	
Answering a Complaint	
Dealing with Losing/Failure	
Dealing with Embarrassment	
Accepting No	
Being Honest	
Completing Assignments/Projects	
Following the School Procedures/Rules	
How not to be the Rule Police	
Applying for a Job	
Completing a Job Application	
Answering Questions during a Job Interview	
Knowing how to use the Restroom	
Knowing how to Participate in Leisure/After School activities	

Chapter 3:

Social-Skill Lessons
Conversations and Getting to Know Others

The best kind of friend is the kind you can sit on a porch swing with, never say a word, then walk away feeling like it was the best conversation that you ever had.

~ *Unknown*

Merriam-Webster's Dictionary defines a conversation as an oral exchange of sentiments, observations, or ideas. Many students have difficulty exchanging information in a conversation. Conversation deficits can affect school and job performance. Relationships can also be adversely affected by poor conversation skills.

The following lesson contains several activities that teachers and other education professionals can use to help their students strengthen these conversation skills.

Interviewing: Asking Questions

Through practicing the interviewing process, students will learn how to ask questions in order to obtain further information from others. Students often need to be taught how to formulate a question.

A Personal Interview

The first interview that a student should conduct is a personal interview. The student asks another person questions that will produce information about the person's life, opinions, and hobbies.

1. What school do you attend?
2. What do you like about school?
3. What sport(s) do you like?
4. When do you go on vacation?
5. Where do you want to work?

After the students develop personal questions for an interview, they should write the questions on index cards.

They can then role-play a personal interview. After a few interviews, they will begin to learn to "extend" the questions.

Example: a. What school do you attend?
b. Where is your school?

Extensions

Students can also complete "character interviews." The person being interviewed can develop a character such as a policeman, a superhero, or a hippie. They can wear hats or use props to help create the character. When answering questions, they should answer as the character would answer. The students are not only learning how to complete interviews but also that people have different interests and opinions.

Taxi Driver Exercise

Many students may become frustrated in a conversation due to limitations in their expressive and spontaneous language. They also may have difficulty with social reciprocity in a conversation. The taxi driver exercise can help to increase these deficits.

One student should be chosen to role-play as the taxi driver. The driver's job is to ask the passenger questions. It may help some students to have cards with question starters written on them. Someone can hold huge cue cards in front of the driver for prompting. Being a driver can be difficult for some students! They have to monitor the conversation more closely than the passenger. Here are some questions the driver could ask the passenger.

1. Where are you going?
2. Why are you going there?
3. What will you do when you get there?
4. When will you need a ride home?

The passenger chooses the character that he will act out such as a king, queen, army man, robot, teacher, robber, cowboy, or rap star. Once he chooses a character, he should answer the questions as if he were that character. Difficulty arises when the passenger has to extend the answers. One-word answers should be acceptable as the student learns to master answering questions.

Completing a Successful Conversation

Once your students have mastered creating and answering questions, they are ready to learn the elements of a successful conversation. Education professionals should emphasize that it takes two actively involved people to make a proper conversation. When a single student dominates the conversation, the conversation becomes a lecture. A lesson should be taught on each element in a conversation. Then, multiple elements of a conversation are grouped into lessons.

Stop and Think before You Begin

Different social scenarios require people to engage in different types of conversations. Before beginning a conversation with someone, a student with social deficits needs to stop and think in order to plan the best way to start. The type of conversation will determine how the student begins. Here are two examples of different types of conversation with prompts of how to begin.

Meeting Someone New

- ✓ You should approach the person by making good eye contact and by facing the other person.
- ✓ Say, "Hello."
- ✓ Then introduce yourself. "I'm _____."
- ✓ If the other person does not introduce himself, ask him his name.

> Speaking to a Close Friend
>
> ✓ You should approach the other person by making good eye contact and by facing the other person.
>
> ✓ Say, "Hello." (Only say hello when you see him for the first time that day.)
>
> ✓ Wait until you receive a response from him before you begin the conversation. If he does not state, "Hello," determine if he said hello nonverbally? (He may nod and smile.)

The same checklist can be used when beginning a conversation with an acquaintance, with someone of the opposite sex, or with an adult.

(When speaking to an adult, beginning the conversation is the same. Students should understand that when they address an adult in a school setting, they should use formal language—example: Ms. Jones.)

Extensions

Students should role-play many different types of conversations. To enhance learning, show them small video clips from movies, television, or from a video modeling resource to reinforce the right and wrong ways to begin conversations. Here are some examples that could be used.

Movie and Television Clips

Confessions of a Teenage Drama Queen—The main character meets a new friend at school while locking her bike on a rack.

Freaky Friday—A teenager introduces her boyfriend to her mother.

Freaks & Geeks (Disk 3)—A boy and his friends meet a new girl in the cafeteria.

Never Been Kissed—The main character introduces herself to three girls in the cafeteria. (This clip shows an inappropriate way to begin a conversation.)

Check the Timing and the Environment

Students should learn to decide if the timing is good for a conversation. They should also consider if the environment is appropriate for the conversation. Frequently, students forget that having a conversation with a peer during class time is inappropriate and inconsiderate of others. If a student has difficulty deciding if the time and environment are ideal, they can always ask the other person's permission to begin the conversation.

Following are some situations that students could practice role-playing. These situation examples are improvisational acting prompts.

Meeting a New Student in Class

A new student is sitting at a table when you walk into class. The tardy bell has not rung yet. It appears to be a good time to talk to the new student. Remember, you have to finish the conversation when the bell rings. When you walk over to the new student, you realize the chair beside him is empty. Ask him if you can sit next to him. If he says yes, he is giving you permission to not only sit next to him but to have a conversation. Once you sit down, you can introduce yourself.

Meeting a New Student in the Hallway

A new student just passed you in the hallway between classes. You turn around to try to catch up with him, but he is walking too fast. Ask yourself, "Is this a good time?"

Speaking to a Close Friend

You have something exciting news to tell your friend, but, you don't want anyone else to know your news. When you finally find your friend, he is talking to five other friends. Is this good timing? What do you do?

Speaking to a Close Friend

The bell rings for lunch and you have not seen your friend today. As you sit down, you see your friend at a different table. You decide to sit next to your friend, since he is sitting by himself. What will you say as you approach your friend? Do you say hello? Do you ask him if you can sit next to him?

Speaking to an Adult

You are sitting in class listening to your teacher's lecture on World War II. Suddenly, you want to tell your teacher about the game that you bought over the weekend. Is it the time and place to have a conversation? What do you do?

Speaking to an Adult

The bell rang and school is out for the day. As you walk down the hallway, you see your science teacher sitting at her desk. You realize that you have a question about your homework assignment. How do you approach your science teacher? Is this good timing?

Extension

Student can view small clips from movies, television, or from a video modeling resource to decide if the characters began a conversation at a good time and environment. The educator should pause the video clip to allow the student to view the facial expressions and body gestures of the characters for further discussions about social cues.

Movie and Television Clips

A Walk to Remember: The female character sits down and visits with a boy on the bus

Sky High: A female character waits for her boyfriend at a restaurant. He does not come, and the waiter starts a conversation with her.

Shrek: Shrek is trying to get away from the donkey as he continues to talk to him.

Putting all of the Elements to a Successful Conversation Together

When the students have learned all the elements of a successful conversation, they should examine these elements visually. By viewing video clips, and acting out skits, they can become social detectives while determining if the characters are following the elements. Here is the list of the elements.

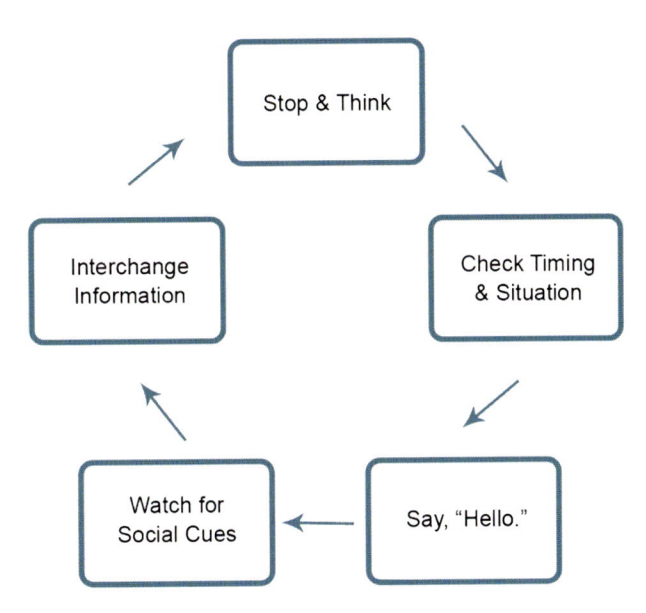

```
        Stop & Think
       ↗           ↘
Interchange      Check Timing
Information      & Situation
       ↑           ↙
   Watch for  ←  Say, "Hello."
   Social Cues
```

The following pages include scripts that can be acted out by the students to determine if the characters followed all of the elements. Discussion should occur after the script has been acted out.

A Three Element Social Skill Program

Aaron & Kevin

(School is over. Kevin and Aaron meet while walking home.)

Aaron: Hi. You're the new kid, who just moved in, aren't you?

Kevin: Yes.

Aaron: Into the big white house with horses?

Kevin: Yes.

Aaron: Austin Fay used to live there.

Kevin: Really?

Aaron: Yea, he used to be my best friend. I met him when I was 5 years old! We had the same teachers. His dad lost his job, and he had to move to Georgia.

Kevin: I'm sorry that he had to move. What is there to do around here?

Aaron: Everyone hangs out at the movie theatre or at the mall.

Kevin: Cool. In Florida, we use to meet at the beach. Gosh, I will miss the beach life! And, seeing babes in bathing suits!!

Aaron: Hey, I am meeting some of my friends at the mall in just a few minutes. Do you want to come? You may not see girls in bathing suits, but there are some good looking ones that work at the mall. I will introduce you to them.

Kevin: Sounds great! Let's go!

Extensions

After the students decide if these characters followed the elements of a conversation, more questions could be discussed.

1. Kevin lived in Florida. Where do you think he moved to?
2. How do you think Aaron felt when his friend Austin moved?
3. How old do you think Austin and Aaron are?
4. Would Kevin use slang (babes) when talking to an adult?

Terra and Amber

(Amber and Terra are enrolled in a ballet class. Amber is a new student to the ballet company.)

Amber: Hi, I'm Amber. Where do I put my dance bag?

Terra: You put your bag on the floor next to the door. Here, I will show you.

Amber: Thank you! I'm not for sure what the dance rules are.

Terra: Don't worry! I will help you. Let me know if you have any questions.

Amber: How many years have you been in ballet?

Terra: This will be my sixth year.

Amber: Wow! You must really love it. This is only my first year.

Terra: Well, my mother says that it keeps me out of trouble. I would love to play soccer instead, but my mother told me that it was a boy's sport.

Amber: I want to become a professional dancer some day. Oh, this must be the dance teacher.

Extensions

1. Did Terra and Amber follow all of the elements to a good conversation?
2. How old do you think they are?
3. Do you think Amber enjoys dancing?
4. Why do you think Terra's mother thinks soccer is only for boys?
5. Do Amber and Terra have anything in common?
6. Do you think they will become friends?

> **Madison and Dillon**
>
> (During lunch, Dillon realizes that Madison is eating with only one friend. He decides to go and talk to her for a few minutes. He stands besides her, and she stops eating to see what he wants.)
>
> **Dillon:** Um.Um.Um.
>
> **Madison:** Hi Dillon.
>
> **Dillon:** Um. Um. Um.
>
> **Madison:** Do you need something?
>
> **Dillon:** No. Um. Can I sit down next to you?
>
> **Madison:** I'm sorry! I have a few more friends who are coming to eat with me.
>
> **Dillon:** Oh, Okay.

Extensions

1. Did Madison and Dillon follow the conversation elements?
2. What should Dillon have done differently?
3. Do you think Madison and Dillon are friends?
4. How do you think Dillon is feeling in this situation?
5. How do you think Madison is feeling in this situation?

Kelley and Bryan

(Kelley and Bryan are at a school dance. Bryan wants to ask Kelley to dance. He walks over to her. She is talking to a group of friends. He stands and waits next to her until she looks at him.)

Bryan: Hi, Kelley.

Kelley: Hi, Bryan.

Bryan: Are you having a good time?

Kelley: Yes! I'm having fun with Samantha and Jeanna. Samantha's mom brought us. How about you?

Bryan: It's okay. I rode with Enrique, but he is with his girlfriend.

Kelley: You can hang out with us if you want too.

Bryan: Thanks!

Kelley: Samantha, Jeanna, this is Bryan. We have science class together.

Bryan: Hi!

Kelley: Can you believe that Ms. Sanders gave us all of that homework for this weekend? I was lucky to have come tonight.

Bryan: Yea, I will be busy this weekend. If you need help give me a call. Do you like to dance?

Kelley: It depends on the song.

Bryan: Do you like this song?

Kelley: Yes.

Bryan: Do you want to go dance then?

Kelley: Okay. Let's go!

Extensions

1. Did Kelley and Bryan follow the conversation elements?
2. How do you think Bryan was feeling?
3. How do you think Kelley was feeling?
4. Were they friends?
5. How do you think Kelley's friends felt when she danced with Bryan?
6. Do you think Kelley wanted to dance with Bryan?

Educators can develop their own scripts to enhance a student's educational program.

Analyzing Video Clips

As students view video clips, they can use the table below to help them analyze the characters' actions.

Movie/Television Series	Did they stop and think?	Is the timing and situation good?	Did they say, "Hello?"	Did they watch the social cues?	Did they take turns talking in the conversation?

*Write Yes/No to answer each question about the movie.

Chapter 4:

Social Skill Lesson: Identifying Feelings in Self and in Others

Feelings or emotions are the universal language and are to be honored.
They are the authentic expression of who you are at your deepest place.

~ Judith Wright

It is vital that the students understand the role that feelings and emotions play when learning appropriate social skills. Unless students understand the emotional role, they will not be able to "connect" socially. Without this understanding, they will have difficulty developing close relationships. This chapter contains several activities that middle school aged students could complete to strengthen their knowledge of feelings about themselves and others.

Using Music, Video Clips and Art to Teach Emotions

Using music, painting, and video clips from movies can enhance lessons on emotions. As students listen to different music genres, they can paint along with the music. Discussions about how the music makes them feel, and why, can help them to understand different emotions. Students can experience how different colors can represent emotions, as well. Video clips that have music to enhance the mood of the scene can be shown. Analyzing the way in which the characters react during the video clip is important for the students to understand the connection between music and emotions.
　　Below is an example of the lesson.

1. Provide students with primary paint colors to use when painting. Paint brushes, sponges, cotton, or objects with different textures can be used.

2. Students should listen to different music genre. Halloween music, rock-n-roll, musical theater, and jazz could be played. The students paint as they listen to the music.

3. Once the music has ended a discussion should take place about how the music made the students feel. Pictures of different facial expressions should be shown.

A Three Element Social Skill Program

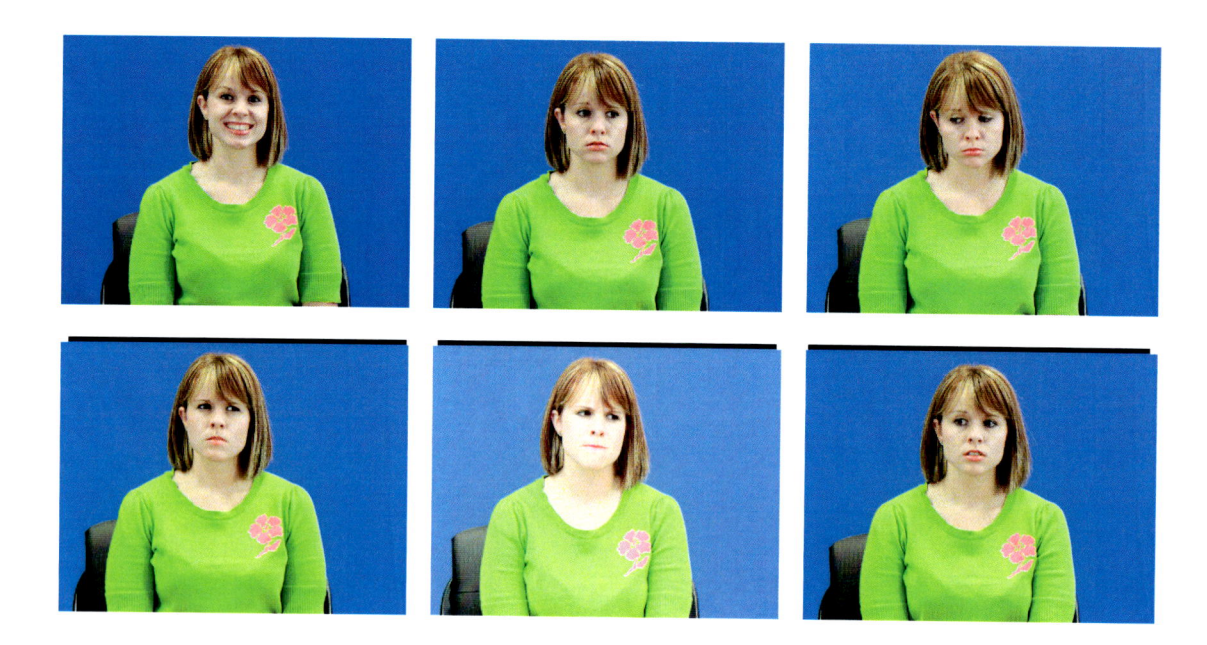

Portrait pictures are better to use than a cartoon drawing of an emotion. Educators can use pictures of themselves. It is important to show the same emotion being expressed by different individuals since facial expressions appear to look different on everyone.

4. A discussion of the paint colors should be completed. Why did a student choose a red color to interpret anger? Students will learn that people use different colors to express different emotions. The color red is usually associated with being angry. The color yellow is usually expressed with being happy. Below is a drawing a child completed while listening to Halloween music.

Extension

To illustrate how emotions can be felt in a movie scene, students should view different movie clips that contain a variation of background music. The music sets the mood of the scene. Example: The music in the movie Jaws was used to scare the audience. Every time the music played, a character in the movie would be eaten by Jaws. The anticipation of the event captivated the audience.

Michelle Henderson

Creating Characters to Teach Emotions

Using hats and props to create different characters is a creative way to teach emotions. Students are given a type of emotion, and then, they create a character based upon that emotion.

This student is displaying the emotion "happy." His character is going to a Fiesta school party.

Here are some additional examples:

1. A student may dress up as a person in jail when portraying a person being scared.
2. A student may dress up as a clown when portraying a person being silly/funny.
3. A student may dress up as a soldier when portraying a person being brave.
4. A student may dress up as a hippie when portraying a person being peaceful.

Different Environments, Situations, and Emotions

> "People with Asperger's Syndrome find the 'land of emotions' to be uncharted territory. In the last few years there has been increasing interest in one of the most important components of social behaviour, namely the communication of emotions or feelings." (Tony Attwood, 1998)

The world can be a confusing place for everyone! Understanding and knowing how to deal with emotions is important for a student with social deficits to understand. Frequently, students will isolate themselves when they become confused and anxious about their environment and the people involved in this environment. Interventions should assist in increasing students "Theory of Mind." This is the ability to recognize and understand thoughts, beliefs, desires, and intentions of other people in order to make sense of their behavior and predict what they are going to do next. (Baron-Cohen, 1995)

Magazines are a wonderful source to begin teaching students about different emotional situations that people experience on a daily basis. Why does someone cry at a wedding? Students can look through magazines to find people who are sad, excited, and angry. Discussions should center on why these people feel the way they do. Students should be asked if they would feel the same way if they were in the same situation.

Watching video clips is another visual strategy that can be used. It is important to freeze frame the character's facial expression so the students can view what the emotion "looks like."

An example of a chart can be used for discussions.

Video Clip	Character?	Situation?	Emotion?

Mirrors are a wonderful tool to use when teaching students different facial expressions. Students should view themselves in the mirror as different situations are read. After the situation is explained, the student should make the facial expression that is appropriate with the situation.

Example: Sally was playing a video game on her computer. Suddenly, she felt something on her arm. She realizes that there is a spider on her arm!

What type of facial expression is she displaying? What emotion is this?

Using Drama to Teach Emotions

Student need to learn that people not only show emotions through facial expressions, but also through body movements. Watching video clips from silent movies are a great way to show non-verbal language. Charlie Chaplin and Mr. Bean have good video footage to show.

After the students have viewed silent movie clips, they should have a turn at making a silent movie that has a commentator telling the story. The students should act out the script as a commentator explains what is happening in the scene. Students should emphasize their own non-verbal language.

Brandon and Cameron

One afternoon, Brandon was completing an assignment in the library. Cameron walks into the library with a CD player. He walks over to Brandon, and slams the CD player onto the table that Brandon is sitting at. Suddenly, Brandon looks up (with a shocked expression on his face). Cameron begins to yell at Brandon since he broke his CD player (flinging his arms in anger). Brandon begins to shake his head no, and begins to explain what happened to the CD player. Cameron did not want to listen, and stomps out of the library leaving the CD player with Brandon (with his arms crossed).

Educators could ask the following questions about the scene.

1. How was Cameron feeling during the scene? How did you know?
2. How was Brandon feeling when Cameron began to yell at him?
3. What do you think Cameron said to Brandon?
4. Do you think Cameron was still angry?

A Three Element Social Skill Program

Amber and Terra

One day after school, Terra was studying for a test in the library. Amber walked into the library, and she walked over to Terra. She decided to sit next to Terra, so she could tell Terra about a party that she was having on Saturday. She was so excited to tell someone! As she sat down, she started describing the party events. Terra gazed from her book, and tried to interrupt Amber. (She placed her finger over her lips to tell Amber that she wanted to study.) Amber did not notice that Terra wanted her to be quiet. Amber continued to talk as Terra crossed her arms across her chest. After a few minutes, Terra closed her book. Amber continued to talk. Being frustrated, Terra stood up. Amber did not make eye contact with Terra as she continued to tell her about the party plans. Quickly, Terra walked away. Amber continued to talk. She did not realize that Terra left the library.

Educators could use these questions about this scene.

1. How did Terra feel when Amber interrupted her studying?

2. How do you think Amber felt when she realized that Terra was no longer sitting next to her?

3. What could Amber have done differently?

Scripts can also be used to determine how situations can make other people feel. Students can change the situation to help others feel better. This activity can help increase empathy towards others.

The Game— Scene 1

Christian and Nick are in school locker room after a baseball game. Christian is feeling defeated after he missed catching the ball. The other team won the game due to Christian's mistake.

Christian: I can't believe I missed the ball! I should have had it!

Nick: Yea, I know. It lost the game for us. The third base runner would not have scored if you had caught it. WE might have won!

Christian: Thanks, I feel worse now! *Christian walks out of the room.*

Nick: What's wrong?

A discussion how Christian felt when his teammate criticized him for his mistake. What could Nick say that would make Christian feel better? Role-play the scene again with the students' suggestions. Below is an example of what Nick could have said.

The Game— Scene 2

Christian and Nick are in school locker room after a baseball game. Christian is feeling defeated after he missed catching the ball. The other team won the game due to Christian's mistake.

Christian: I can't believe I missed the ball! I should have had it!

Nick: Yea, but mistakes can happen! I missed the ball several times in the game too.

Christian: But, you did not lose the game!

Nick: Neither did you! We work as a team. You were not the only one who made a mistake. Do you want to go get our free coke?

Extensions

Students can practice acting out emotions by reciting poetry. Since poetry is rhythmic, students can recite poems easily with emotions. They can also practice strengthening their pitch and tone of voice. Have you ever heard anyone recite "Twinkle Twinkle Little Star" displaying anger?

Learning about Anger

Students should learn that everyone expresses emotions differently. Anger is an emotion that everyone feels, but it is how they *deal* with the anger that is important. Range, fury, resentment, and indignation are synonyms of anger.

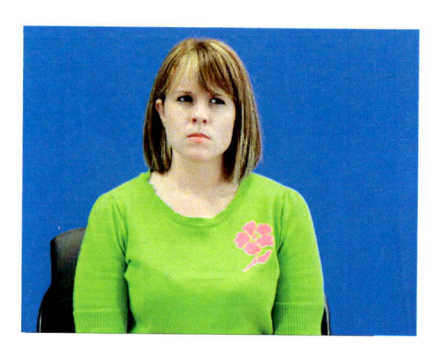

Educators should teach students that there are different degrees of anger. A concrete way to illustrate different degrees of anger is by using a thermometer. Placing a thermometer in water which is room temperature illustrates a non-degree of anger. Taking temperature of hot water, illustrates a high degree of anger.

A thermometer that illustrates 0 degrees to 10 degrees should be used when discussing what situation makes a student feels at the different degrees. Educators should teach students what happens physically when a student is feeling at the different degrees.

Examples are shown below.

1 degree— When a person is feeling a 1 degree of anger, he is not feeling anything physically. The activity the person is doing is not causing him to be angry.

5 degrees— When a person is feeling 5 degrees of anger, he is beginning to sweat; his heart is beating faster; and his muscles are beginning to tighten. At 5 degrees of anger, the person is still able to do relaxing strategies to decrease his anger.

10 degrees— When a person is feeling 10 degrees of anger, he is sweating; his heart is beating fast and hard; he is not able to breathe, and his muscles are tight. At 10 degrees of anger, a person cannot think logically, and becomes aggressive. He will need time to himself before he can apply strategies to help him decrease his anger.

Michelle Henderson

Extensions

Showing a video clip from the movie Hulk could be used to illustrate the different degrees of anger. At the beginning of the scene, the main character is working at the computer with no emotion. He begins to reflect on previous experiences that begin to make him feel angry. Trying to relax, he walks away from his computer. Suddenly, he trips over a mop bucket in the hallway. He can no longer control his anger, and morphs into the Hulk.

Chapter 5:

Social Skill Lesson: How to Deal with a Bullying Attempt

"Autistic children are often tormented and rejected by their classmates simply because they are different and stand out from the crowd. Thus, in the playground or on the way to school one can often see an autistic child at the centre of a jeering horde of little urchins. The child himself may be hitting out in blind fury or crying helplessly. In either case he is defenseless."

~ Hans Asperger ([1944] 1991)

Being a victim of a bullying attempt is devastating to any student, and can create life-long affects. Students who display social deficits become vulnerable to these bullying attempts. Usually, victims to these attempts are passive, anxious, quiet, sensitive, or unusual in many ways. It is important for educators to teach strategies to student on how to deal with these bullying attempts. Schools systems also need to train educators on procedure and policies that can be followed when a situation occurs. Gray recommends creating a map of the child's world and identifying places where the child is vulnerable to, or safe from, acts of bullying. Some areas can then receive more supervision from staff knowledgeable in how to monitor and prevent bullying, and more safe-havens can be created. (Gray, 2004 a)

Different Forms of Bullying

Learning the different forms of bullying is important for students to learn. Physical bullying, Word bullying, Social Bullying, and Cyber Bulling are the different types of bullying. If students understand why someone would choose to be a part of a bullying attempt, they may realize this person is making a poor choice. These victims will become empowered to do something.

1. Physical Bullying— When a student kicks, punch, spits, pulls at others clothing, shoves, and trips; he is participating in physical bullying.

2. Word Bullying— Using words, or non-verbal language are elements of word bullying. Cursing, yelling, threatening, and making someone feel inadequate are examples of someone participating in word bullying.

3. Social Bullying— Using a group of peers to make someone feel bad is a form of social bullying. Spreading rumors, shunning, gossiping are examples of social bullying.

4. <u>Cyber Bullying</u>— This is the newest form of bullying. When others use technology to make someone feel inadequate, they are displaying cyber bullying. Students who e-mail inappropriate messages or pictures are participating in cyber bullying. Teenagers are prone to becoming victims to cyber bullying if someone takes an inappropriate picture of them, and sends this picture to others.

Using video clips from movies that illustrate the different types of bullying, students can learn what each type "looks" like. Once they understand each type of bulling, educators should teach different strategies these students can use if they become victims of a bullying attack.

Movie Clip	Physical Bullying?	Verbal Bullying?	Social Bullying?	Cyber Bullying?

This chart is an example of what educators can use when viewing the video clips. Below is a list of movies that have good examples of different types of bullying.

1. Freaks & Geeks
2. Shreaderman
3. Shark Boy and Lava Girl
4. Drama Queen
5. Never Been Kissed
6. How to Eat Fried Worms
7. Jumanji
8. Bullies are a Pain

Strategies to Use

Students will feel empowered if they know strategies to use when they become victims of someone's bullying attempt. They should practice these strategies in different environments so the knowledge of these strategies will generalize. Educators should have a campus plan on how to help students deal with bullying. It is vital that students know there is a "safe" place for them to go. Assigning a teacher to students will allow them to bond and feel safe with him/her. Here are some key elements that students should learn when dealing with bullying.

1. Know that you are okay. Do not believe what a bully tells you!
2. Believe in yourself.
3. Use humor.
4. Do not give the person who is bullying any power! Walk away and go find an adult.

Matt and the Bullying Attempt

Matt is sitting in a classroom alone. He has his pencils and textbook on his desk. Sam and a group of boys enter the classroom.

Sam: Hey, Matt! Did you do your homework last night? (Sam approaches Matt's desk.)

Matt: Yes, I stayed up late and did it on my computer. Did you know that a careful analysis of the process of observation in atomic physics has show that the subatomic particles..

Sam: I don't care! That is so stupid! (Sam pushes Matt's books off of the desk. The other boys laugh.)

Matt: (Matt puts his head down.)

Sam: (Sam kicks Matt's books across the room.)

Students should role-play the script. Then, discuss the questions below. Educators may choose to play the role of Sam.

1. What type of bullying took place?
2. What should Matt have done when Sam began to yell at him?
3. Should Matt be in the classroom all by himself?

After the discussion, students should role-play a strategy that Matt could use.

Matt and the Bullying Attempt #2

Matt is sitting in a classroom alone. He has his pencils and textbook on his desk. Sam and a group of boys enter the classroom.

Sam: Hey, Matt! Did you do your homework last night? (Sam approaches Matt's desk.)

Matt: Yes, I stayed up late and did it on my computer. Did you know that a careful analysis of the process of observation in atomic physics has show that the subatomic particles..

Sam: I don't care! That is so stupid! (Sam pushes Matt's books off of the desk. The other boys laugh.)

Matt: Stop! Leave me alone! (Matt gets up from his desk, and walks out of the classroom.)

Sam: (Sam kicks Matt's books across the room.)

Questions:

1. What did Matt do differently?
2. Do you think he will go back into an empty classroom again?
3. What do you think he did once he left the classroom?

Educators should teach students that it is okay to report to the teacher about an incident. Carol Gray's bullying program teaches the difference between reporting an incident, and tattling on someone. Students need to report an incident to a teacher if they feel that they are in danger, hurt, or embarrassed. When students tattle on someone, usually they are trying to get him/her into trouble. Below are scripts that could be used for the students to practice reporting a bullying attempt.

Matt Reports a Bullying Attempt

Matt walks into the counselor's office.

Matt: Ms. Tyson, can I talk to you for a few minutes?

Ms. Tyson: Sure Matt, come in!

Matt: I need to tell you about something that just happened.

Ms. Tyson: Okay. Tell me what happened. I can tell that you are upset.

Matt: I was sitting in my science classroom waiting for everyone to get there. Sam walked into the room with Mike and Brandon. They walked over to my desk. Sam asked me if I had done my homework. I told that I had, and I was trying to tell him what I learned from my homework. He told me that I was stupid! Then, he pushed my books off of my desk.

Ms. Tyson: What did you do?

Matt: I told them to stop, and ran out of the room!

Ms. Tyson: You did the right thing. You do not deserve being treated this way. I am so glad that you came to talk to me. I will talk to the boys about what happened. Please come talk to me again if it happens again. I would suggest not being in the classroom by yourself. I would wait to sit down when the teacher is in the room.

Chapter 6:

Social Skill Lesson: Preparing for Vocational and Career Plans

Tony Attwood has commented, "I have always been impressed by their patience and ingenuity in achieving abilities others acquire without a second thought." Many students who have been diagnosed with Asperger's syndrome have obsessions and fascinations with various topics. Whatever their particular facination, educators should help students channel their talents and interests into vocational or career plans. This chapter demonstrates how educators can guide students into making future plans. Temple Grandin describes a constructive application of one of her interests:

> Another of my fixations was automatic sliding doors in supermarkets and airports. A teacher might wonder, "How can I use math, science, and English in a door fixation?" At the elementary level, tasks could be simple, such as requesting the door company to send its catalog. Adults might think such a catalog boring but the autistic child with a door fixation would find it fascinating. Math and geography could be involved by asking the child to find the door company on a map and measure the miles to it from the school. (Grandin, 1998)

Developing a news segment, cooking show, or informative show are different ways students can give information about a topic in which they are interested. The camera becomes a vital tool for the students to be able to express themselves.

Understanding Talents

Students should have an understanding of their strengths and weaknesses when determining what jobs and careers they should pursue. Completing research on what type of jobs are available will assist students to make a vocational plan. After completing the research, students should choose a job that they want to pursue. Students will understand what type of talent and qualifications a person will have to be successful when they complete a job application and complete a mock interview. An example of a job application that could be used can be found at the end of this chapter.

Mock Interviews

A creative way for students to understand that each job consist of different qualifications is for educators to set up a "character" mock interview. Students play the role of a character applying for a job that they would *not* apply for. Example: A student acts as a person applying for a farm/ranch job, when he does not have knowledge about the workings of a farm. The person interviewing should ask questions that pertain to the job.

"What type of farm experience do you have? "

"Are you familiar with the different types of irrigation?"

"Have you ever worked around animals?"

"Why do you want to get a job on a farm?"

Students will not only have fun completing character mock interviews, but they will also learn about the qualifications that people need to have for different jobs. Once students complete the character mock interviews, they should be ready to participate in a "reality based" interview. Students should choose a job that they are interested in applying for, and complete a job application. Educators should complete a lesson on the correct way to complete a professional resume and application. The reality based interview questions are similar to the character interview questions. The interview should also consist of questions about the student's resume and application. Students should dress professionally for the interview.

Now for the Real World!

Once students have completed the mock interviews, an educator or a job coach should assist the students in making an appointment for a job interview in the community. Students might be able to complete a mock interview, but problems may arise when these students become anxious interviewing with a new professional. Educators should continue to support students until they are self-confident during the interviewing process. Professionals who interview the students should be contacted to determine how the students did during the interview.

A Three Element Social Skill Program

Job Application

Personal Information

Full Name	
Street Address	
City, State, Zip Code	
Home Phone #	
Cell Phone #	
E-Mail	

1. Are you eligible to work in the United States?

   Yes _____   No _____

2. If you are under age 18, do you have an employment/age certificate?

   Yes _____   No _____

3. Have you been convicted of or pleaded no contest to a felony within the last five years?

   Yes _____   No _____

   If yes, explain. _____

Position

4. Which position are you applying for? _____

5. Days and Times available

Day	Time
Sunday	
Monday	
Tuesday	
Wednesday	
Thursday	
Friday	
Saturday	

6. When you can start working? _____

Education History

Name & Address of School	Degree/Diploma	Graduation Date

7. Please list your Skills and Qualifications: Licenses, Skills, Training, and Awards

_____
_____
_____
_____
_____
_____
_____
_____
_____
_____
_____
_____
_____
_____
_____
_____
_____
_____
_____

A Three Element Social Skill Program

Employment History

Present or last Position:	
Employer:	
Address:	
Supervisor:	
Phone:	
E:Mail:	
Position Title:	
From: To:	
Responsibilities:	
Reason for leaving:	

References:

Name:	Address:	Phone #:
Name:	Address:	Phone#:
Name:	Address:	Phone #:
Name:	Address:	Phone #:

I certify that information contained in this application is true and complete. I understand that false information may be grounds for not hiring me or for immediate termination of employment at any point in the future if I am hired. I authorize the verification of any or all information listed above.

Signature _____

Date _____

References for Chapters

American Phsychiatric Association, . (2000). *DSM-IV-TR- Diagnostic and statistical manual of mental disorders.* (Vol. 4, Ed.). American Psychiatric Association Publishing Incorporated.

Attwood, T. (1998). *Asperger's Syndrome.* (Vol. 1, Ed.). LondonN1 9JB, UK: Jessica Kingsley Publishers.

Attwood, T. (2007). *The Complete Guide to Asperger's Syndrome.* London, Jessica Kingsley Publishers.

Baron-Cohen, S. (1995). Mind Blindness; An Essay on Autism and Theory of Mind. Cambridge, MA; MIT Press

Bellini, S., Akullian, J., and Hopf, A. (2007). Increasing social engagement in young children with autism spectrum disorders using video self-modeling. *School Psychology Review, 36* pp. 80-90.

Bellini, S., and Akullian, J. (2007). A meta-analysis of video modeling and video self-modeling interventions for children and adolescents. *Exceptional Children, 73* pp. 261-284.

Gray, (2004,). Gray's guide to bullying part I-III. *The morning News pp. 1-60.*

In *In IU New Room; Indiana University.* (2007). (chap. newinfoWatching videos can help children with autism learn social skills) from http://newsinfo.iu.edu/news/page/normal/5254.html

Movie/Television Series References

Trevor Romain: Bullies Are a Pain in the Brain.

Adamson, A. *Shrek (Full Screen Single Disc Edition).*

Dolman, B. *How to Eat Fried Worms (New Line Platinum Series).*

Gosnell, R. *Never Been Kissed.*

Holland, S. (2007). *Shredderman Rules.*

Johnston, J. *Jumanji.*

Lee, A. *Hulk.*

Mitchell, M. *Sky High (Full Screen Edition).*

Rodriguez, R. *The Adventures of Sharkboy and Lavagirl (2D Version Only).*

Shankman, A. *A Walk to Remember*

Spielberg, S. *Jaws.*

Sugarman, S. *Confessions of a Teenage Drama Queen.*

Waters, M. *Freaky Friday.*